Get Around

for Fun

Get Around
for Fun

by Lee Sullivan Hill

Carolrhoda Books, Inc./Minneapolis

For my son Colin, with love.
—Mom

For more information about the photographs in this book, see the Photo Index on pages 30–32.

The photographs in this book are reproduced through the courtesy of: © Buddy Mays/Travel Stock, cover, pp. 1, 17; © Eugene G. Schulz, p. 2; © Glenn Randall, p. 5; © Bob Firth/Firth PhotoBank, pp. 6, 8, 19, 26, 28; © Robert Fried/Robert Fried Photography, pp. 7, 9, 10, 13, 14, 15, 18, 24, 27; © Sophie Dauwe/Robert Fried Photography, pp. 11, 21; © Richard Cummins, pp. 12, 16, 23; © VSOE Ltd., p. 20; © Howard Ande, p. 22; © David F. Clobes/David F. Clobes Stock Photography, p. 25; © Jerry Hennen, p. 29.

Carolrhoda Books, Inc.
A Division of the Lerner Publishing Group
241 First Avenue North, Minneapolis, MN 55401 U.S.A.

Website address: www.lernerbooks.com

Library of Congress Cataloging-in-Publication Data

Hill, Lee Sullivan, 1958–
    Get around for fun / by Lee Sullivan Hill.
        p. cm. — (A Get around book)
    Includes index.
    Summary: Describes how people choose different ways to use
transportation for fun, depending on setting, circumstances, and
personal preference.
    ISBN 1-57505-312-8
    1. Transportation—Juvenile literature. [1. Transportation.]
I. Title. II. Series: Hill, Lee Sullivan, 1958–   Get around book.
HE152.H55   1999
388—dc21   98-46516

Manufactured in the United States of America
1 2 3 4 5 6 – JR – 04 03 02 01 00 99

Soar over mountains. Glide across the sky.
Transportation takes you from here to there—
sometimes just for fun.

So put on a helmet and whiz across the snow.
Snowmobiles make it fun to get around in the winter.

But what if you don't like cold weather? A camel ride in the sun might be better.

Fun means many different things. It depends upon your point of view. Some people love to zoom around a track. Go-carts race and roar.

Other people stroll over rocky trails. Hikers love pine trees and lakes.

Would you rather ride a float in a holiday parade . . .

or float on a lake in a dragon boat? Some people have fun in a crowd. Others like quiet time with friends.

Up high in the air is fun for some. Rainbow balloons rise and float away.

Down deep underwater is better for others. You can swim eye to eye with fish. Wear an air tank on your back to help you breathe.

Race car drivers like to go fast. They speed around at two hundred miles an hour!

Carriage drivers go more slowly. Even at a trot, horses move only about fifteen miles an hour.

There are many kinds of transportation, many kinds of fun. Your choice might depend on the weather. Windsurf when it's sunny and warm . . .

or cross-country ski when it's cold. Push and glide,
push and glide. Skis slip over the snow.

Where do you want your fun to take you? Motorcycles carry people to faraway places. Saddlebags hold toothbrushes and clothes.

Dirt bikes stay closer to home. They aren't built to run
on roads. People ride them at rallies or on trails.

How much time do you have for your fun? On vacation, you might go by train. Some trains have fold-down beds where you can sleep the night away.

If you only have a Saturday morning, try a bike hike.
You can pedal down roads and over fields.

Do you live in a city by the water? Climb aboard a tour boat. Find a place at the rail and watch the sights go by.

Or do you live way out in the country? Paddle on a lake in a silver canoe. Slip past lily pads by the shore.

Transportation can take you on all kinds of adventures. Pick your way up icy mountains.

Or wander on the water in a sailboat.

You could try something that you've never done before.
Zip across a frozen lake in an iceboat.

Or learn to ride a horse. You might have so much fun
that you want to ride forever!

What is *your* idea of fun? Would you ski to the bottom of a snowy hill? Or would you sled down with a friend?

Sometimes it doesn't matter where you go.
Transportation makes the going fun.

Photo Index

Cover Riders go up, down, and around on this roller coaster in San Antonio, Texas. The designers planned the ups and downs on a small scale so that children would have fun, not be scared out of their wits.

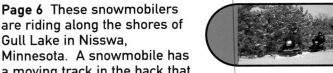

Page 6 These snowmobilers are riding along the shores of Gull Lake in Nisswa, Minnesota. A snowmobile has a moving track in the back that pushes it along. Skis in the front keep the snowmobile from sinking too far into the snow.

Page 1 This girl uses a sit-on-top kayak near Folsom, California. This type of kayak is designed for gentle waters. Kayaks that run rapids in swift rivers have closed tops to keep the water out.

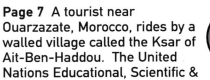

Page 7 A tourist near Ouarzazate, Morocco, rides by a walled village called the Ksar of Ait-Ben-Haddou. The United Nations Educational, Scientific & Cultural Organization (UNESCO) has named the Ksar a World Heritage Site to help preserve it.

Page 2 An unusual vehicle carries these students home from school in Jaipur, India. For students who can afford it, a tourist coach is a fun, quick way to get home at the end of the day.

Page 8 This go-cart driver is zooming around a track in Cottage Grove, Minnesota. A gasoline-powered engine similar to a lawnmower's makes the miniature car roar.

Page 5 The Rocky Mountains tower behind a hang glider at the Telluride Hang Gliding Festival in Colorado. When air currents are heated by the sun, they rise from the valley, carrying the glider like a soaring eagle.

Page 9 These hikers are near Gstaad, Switzerland. One is using a walking stick for balance. Farther up in the Swiss Alps, where the trails grow steeper, walking sticks help even more.

 **Page 10** Mexican American children enjoy a Cinco de Mayo parade in the Mission District of San Francisco, California. This holiday celebrates Mexico's defeat of French forces at the Battle of Puebla on May 5, 1862.

 **Page 11** Family and friends spend time together at Black Dragon Pool Park in Lijiang, Yunnan Province, China. Dragons are powerful symbols of good luck in Chinese culture.

 **Page 12** Temecula, California, holds a Balloon and Wine Festival every year. Balloonists rise up in the sky by heating air with propane heaters. They come down by letting the air cool.

 **Page 13** This scuba diver is swimming down deep in the Caribbean Sea near the Cayman Islands. The underwater camera helps the diver capture pictures of fish that inhabit the warm, salty water.

 **Page 14** This classic 1972 M20 is running in the Monterey Historic Automobile Races at Laguna Seca Raceway in California. The M20 won many Canadian American series races in the 1960s and 1970s.

Page 15 Tourists enjoy a carriage ride near Neuschwanstein Palace in Bavaria, Germany. The horses walk at a speed of three or four miles per hour. The driver directs his team with his voice and hands.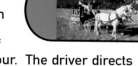

Page 16 Southern California has miles of coastline along the Pacific Ocean and warm weather all year round. This windsurfer is near the town of San Simeon and the California Sea Otter Game Refuge.

Page 17 Cross-country skiers love the cold, snowy weather in Wyoming. This photo was taken at the border of two national parks, Yellowstone and Grand Teton.

Page 18 Two people are riding this motorcycle on Utah Route 12. Touring motorcycles are built to be comfortable and reliable rather than fast.

Page 19 Racers are competing at a rally in Grantsburg, Wisconsin. Dirt bikes are built to travel over rough ground. They have knobby tires that grip the dirt and strong suspensions that can handle bumps.

Page 20 The famous luxury trains of the Orient Express carry passengers across the countryside of Europe and Asia. This train is on its way to Venice, Italy, traveling through the Pettnew-Arlberg Pass in the Austrian Alps.

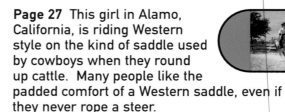

Page 25 This three-masted, wooden sailboat wanders the waters of Lake Superior from its home port of Bayfield, Wisconsin. It is a replica, or a new boat built to look old, of a schooner. The boat measures 54 feet long and 16 feet wide.

Page 21 A boy pauses during his bike ride to smile for a photographer in Lhundup County, Lhassa, Tibet. Bicycles are popular the whole world over, from the mountains of Tibet to the streets of your town.

Page 26 Lake Minnetonka, near Minneapolis, Minnesota, can freeze several feet thick in the winter. This iceboat, pushed along by the wind, skims across the surface on thin steel blades. The huts in the background keep ice fishers warm.

Page 22 This tour boat in Chicago, Illinois, was once used by firefighters. It cruises along the Chicago River—under bridges, between skyscrapers, and past the Centennial Fountain.

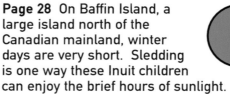

Page 27 This girl in Alamo, California, is riding Western style on the kind of saddle used by cowboys when they round up cattle. Many people like the padded comfort of a Western saddle, even if they never rope a steer.

Page 23 This group is paddling in Union Bay near Seattle, Washington. Their silver canoes are made of aluminum, a light, strong metal. Other kinds of canoes are made of wood, fiberglass, or birch bark.

Page 28 On Baffin Island, a large island north of the Canadian mainland, winter days are very short. Sledding is one way these Inuit children can enjoy the brief hours of sunlight.

Page 24 This hiker in the Canadian Rockies near Jasper, Alberta, has come prepared with warm clothing, heavy boots, and an ice pick.

Page 29 This family's donkey looks quite patient with its riders. The children live in the village of Santa Elena, Mexico, across the Rio Grande from Big Bend, Texas.

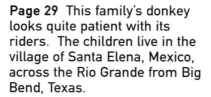